SCIENCE BEHIND THE COLORS
PARROTS

by Alicia Z. Klepeis

pogo

Ideas for Parents and Teachers

Pogo Books let children practice reading informational text while introducing them to nonfiction features such as headings, labels, sidebars, maps, and diagrams, as well as a table of contents, glossary, and index.

Carefully leveled text with a strong photo match offers early fluent readers the support they need to succeed.

Before Reading

- "Walk" through the book and point out the various nonfiction features. Ask the student what purpose each feature serves.
- Look at the glossary together. Read and discuss the words.

Read the Book

- Have the child read the book independently.
- Invite him or her to list questions that arise from reading.

After Reading

- Discuss the child's questions. Talk about how he or she might find answers to those questions.
- Prompt the child to think more. Ask: Did you know about parrots before reading this book? What more would you like to learn about them?

Pogo Books are published by Jump!
5357 Penn Avenue South
Minneapolis, MN 55419
www.jumplibrary.com

Copyright © 2022 Jump! International copyright reserved in all countries. No part of this book may be reproduced in any form without written permission from the publisher.

Library of Congress Cataloging-in-Publication Data

Names: Klepeis, Alicia, 1971- author.
Title: Parrots / Alicia Z. Klepeis.
Description: Minneapolis, MN: Jump!, Inc., [2022]
Series: Science behind the colors
Includes index. | Audience: Ages 7-10
Identifiers: LCCN 2021034363 (print)
LCCN 2021034364 (ebook)
ISBN 9781636903828 (hardcover)
ISBN 9781636903835 (paperback)
ISBN 9781636903842 (ebook)
Subjects: LCSH: Parrots—Juvenile literature.
Parrots—Color—Juvenile literature.
Classification: LCC QL696.P7 K54 2022 (print)
LCC QL696.P7 (ebook) | DDC 598.7/1—dc23
LC record available at https://lccn.loc.gov/2021034363
LC ebook record available at https://lccn.loc.gov/2021034364

Editor: Eliza Leahy
Designer: Emma Bersie

Photo Credits: Eric Isselee/Shutterstock, cover; Butterfly Hunter/Shutterstock, 1; cynoclub/Shutterstock, 3; LifetimeStock/Shutterstock, 4; Martin Pelanek/Shutterstock, 5; Gabbro/Alamy, 6-7t; Charles Bergman/Shutterstock, 6-7b; Tim Burrett/Shutterstock, 8-9; Alex Hyde/Nature Picture Library, 10-11; Nynke van Holten/Shutterstock, 12; Rosa Jay/Shutterstock, 13; Monthira/Shutterstock, 14-15tl; Jearu/Shutterstock, 14-15tr; sunipix55/Shutterstock, 14-15bl; Tessa Palmer/Shutterstock, 14-15br; Gerard Lacz Images/SuperStock, 16; BMJ/Shutterstock, 17; Stephen Belcher/Minden Pictures/SuperStock, 18-19; Meg Forbes/Shutterstock, 20-21; Passakorn Umpornmaha/Shutterstock, 23.

Printed in the United States of America at Corporate Graphics in North Mankato, Minnesota.

TABLE OF CONTENTS

CHAPTER 1
Birds of Many Colors 4

CHAPTER 2
Parrot Pigments 12

CHAPTER 3
Messages in Feathers 16

ACTIVITIES & TOOLS
Try This! 22
Glossary 23
Index 24
To Learn More 24

CHAPTER 1
BIRDS OF MANY COLORS

What **intelligent** bird comes in every color of the rainbow? It is a parrot!

cockatoo

There are more than 350 parrot **species**. Parakeets and lovebirds are kinds of parrots. So are macaws and cockatoos.

CHAPTER 1

Parrots come in many colors and sizes. The buff-faced pygmy parrot is mostly green and yellow. It is the size of a human finger!

The hyacinth macaw is bright blue. It is more than three feet (0.9 meters) tall!

DID YOU KNOW?

Parrots have four toes. Two point forward. Two point backward. This helps them hold onto branches and climb trees!

 CHAPTER 1

buff-faced pygmy parrot

hyacinth macaws

CHAPTER 1

Parrots are **omnivores**. Most eat fruit, flowers, and insects.

Their beaks are super strong. They easily crack open seeds and nuts.

CHAPTER 1

Most parrots live in warm areas. Many live in rain forests. Some live in grasslands.

No matter where they live, parrots live in **flocks**. Some can have as many as 1,000 birds. When they fly by, it is a burst of color!

TAKE A LOOK!

Where do parrots live? Take a look!

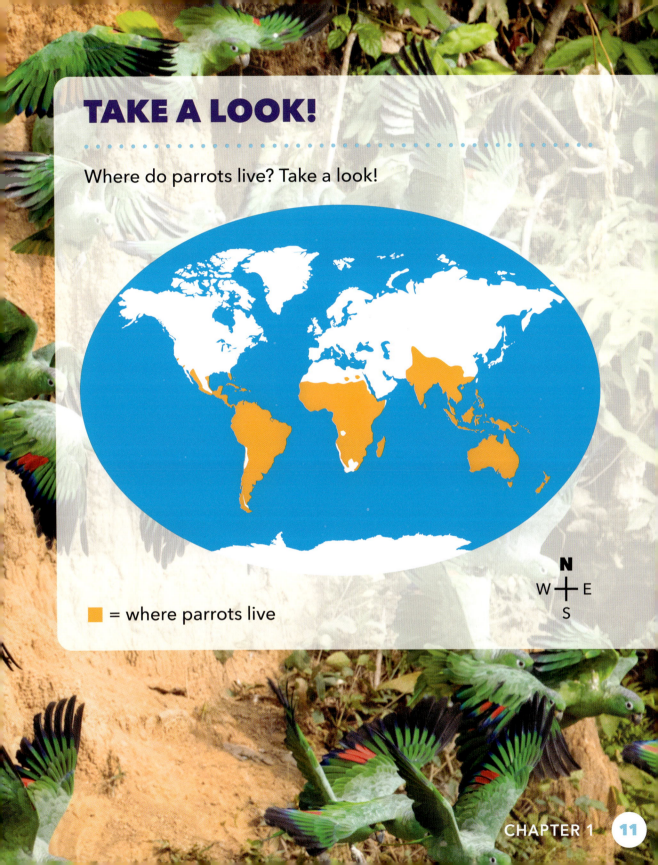

■ = where parrots live

CHAPTER 1   11

CHAPTER 2
PARROT PIGMENTS

Parrots don't begin life with colorful feathers. Parrot **chicks** have fluffy **down** when they hatch. It is gray or white. These colors act as **camouflage**. They help chicks hide from **predators**.

down

Adult feathers start growing in after three weeks. It can take four years for parrots to grow their full colors.

adult feathers

CHAPTER 2 13

Parrots' bodies make **pigments**. These are often what give their feathers color. They can be many different colors, including red, pink, orange, and yellow.

DID YOU KNOW?

The way light **reflects** off feathers can also change color. Most green parrot feathers have yellow pigments. These feathers can also reflect blue light. The yellow pigment and blue light mix to look green.

rosy-faced lovebird

ring-necked parakeet

CHAPTER 2 15

CHAPTER 3
MESSAGES IN FEATHERS

Bright feathers can warn predators to stay away. They can warn other parrots, too. Female eclectus parrots use their feathers this way. They warn others to stay away from their nests.

Bright colors can help camouflage, too. Green feathers blend in with leaves. They help parrots hide from predators, such as snakes and monkeys.

CHAPTER 3

Bright colors help some parrots choose **mates**. In some species, duller colors mean the parrot is more likely to be sick. Brighter feathers show that a bird is healthy.

Some male parrots, like the kakapo, **strut** or dance to show off their colors and **impress** females.

DID YOU KNOW?

In the bird world, females are often duller than males. But not female parrots. Most female parrots are also bright.

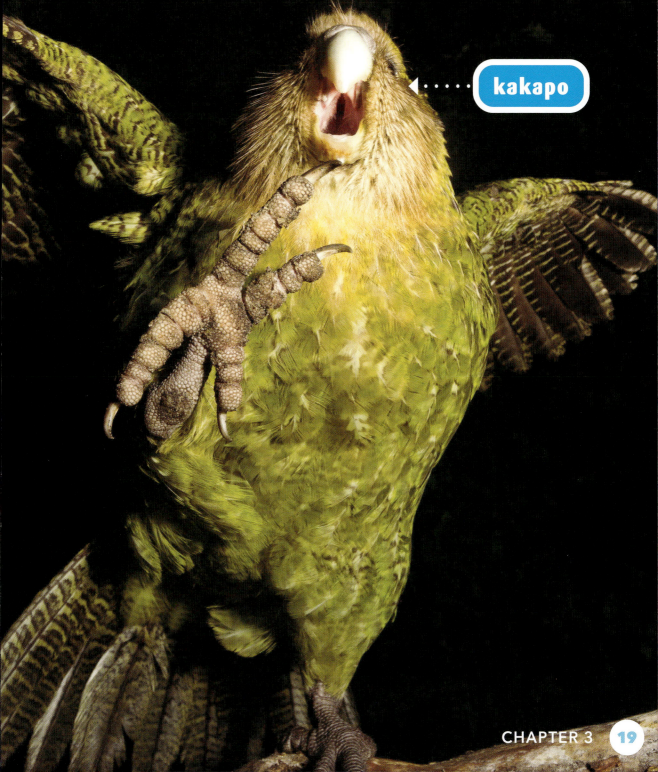
CHAPTER 3

These beautiful birds use their colors in many ways. Their bright feathers help them both hide and stand out.

Have you ever seen a parrot? What colors were its feathers?

CHAPTER 3

ACTIVITIES & TOOLS

TRY THIS!

COLORS IN NATURE

Parrots use their colors to hide and stand out. See how colors help them in this activity!

What You Need:
- white paper
- pencil
- ruler
- scissors
- markers or crayons
- notebook

1. On a sheet of paper, draw four squares. Each should be about 3 × 3 inches (roughly 7.5 × 7.5 centimeters).
2. Cut out the squares.
3. Choose four colors of parrots that you saw in this book. Color each square a different color.
4. Go outside. Choose one square. See if you can find something that the color blends in with. For example, are there flowers or leaves that blend in with a square you made?
5. Repeat Step 3 with the remaining squares.
6. Record the results of what each square best blended in with.
7. Now see what backgrounds make the squares stand out. What do you notice?

GLOSSARY

camouflage: A disguise or natural coloring that allows animals to hide by making them look like their surroundings.

chicks: Young birds.

down: The soft feathers that form the first covering of a bird.

flocks: Groups of birds of one kind that live, travel, or feed together.

impress: To make someone or something feel admiration or respect.

intelligent: Quick to understand, think, and learn.

mates: The breeding partners of a pair of animals.

omnivores: Animals that eat both plants and meat.

pigments: Substances that give color to something.

predators: Animals that hunt other animals for food.

reflects: Throws back heat, light, or sound from a surface.

species: One of the groups into which similar animals and plants are divided.

strut: To walk with a swagger or in a proud way.

ACTIVITIES & TOOLS

INDEX

beaks 9
buff-faced pygmy parrot 6
camouflage 12, 17
chicks 12
climb 6
cockatoos 5
eat 9
eclectus parrots 16
feathers 12, 13, 14, 16, 17, 18, 21
female 16, 18
flocks 10
fly 10
grasslands 10

hyacinth macaw 6
kakapo 18
male 18
mates 18
nests 16
parakeets 5
pigments 14
predators 12, 16, 17
rain forests 10
sick 18
sizes 6
species 5, 18
toes 6

TO LEARN MORE

Finding more information is as easy as 1, 2, 3.
❶ Go to www.factsurfer.com
❷ Enter "parrots" into the search box.
❸ Choose your book to see a list of websites.

24 ACTIVITIES & TOOLS